BREAKOUT BIOGRAPHIES

ELON MUSK

Engineer
and Inventor
for the Future

Sarah Machajewski

PowerKiDS
press

New York

Published in 2018 by The Rosen Publishing Group, Inc.
29 East 21st Street, New York, NY 10010

First Edition

Editor: Elizabeth Krajnik
Book Design: Tanya Dellaccio

Photo Credits: Cover Pascal Le Segretain/Getty Images Entertainment/Getty Images; cover, back cover, pp. 1, 3, 4, 6, 8, 10, 12, 14, 16, 18, 20, 22, 24, 26, 28, 30–32 ninanaina/Shutterstock.com; p. 5 Brian Dowling/Getty Images Entertainment/Getty Images; p. 7 (top) Taina Sohlman/ Shutterstock.com; p. 7 (bottom) Mike Windle/Getty Images Entertainment/Getty Images; p. 9 (top) Joe Corrigan/Getty Images Entertainment/Getty Images; pp. 9 (bottom), 13 (top) Justin Sullivan/ Getty Images News/Getty Images; p. 11 (top) David Paul Morris/Bloomberg/Getty Images; p. 11 (bottom) Axel Koester/Corbis Historical/Getty Images; p. 13 (bottom) Patrick T. Fallon/Bloomberg/ Getty Images; p. 15 (top) Kevork Djansezian/Getty Images News/Getty Images; pp. 15 (bottom), 17 (top) Paul Sakuma/AP Images; p. 17 (bottom) Andrew Harner/Bloomberg/Getty Images; p. 19 Brendan Hoffman/Bloomberg/Getty Images; p. 21 (top) Bruce Weaver/AFP/Getty Images; p. 21 (bottom) Tim Peake/ESA/NASA/Getty Images News/Getty Images; p. 23 (top) Scott Olson/ Getty Images News/Getty Images; p. 23 (bottom) https://commons.wikimedia.org/wiki/ File:N.Tesla.JPG; p. 25 (top) Jag_cz/Shutterstock.com; p. 25 (bottom) VCG/Visual China Group/ Getty Images; p. 27 (top) Mark Von Holden/AP Images; p. 27 (bottom) Jennie Book/Shutterstock.com; p. 29 Jason Merritt/Getty Images Entertainment/Getty Images.

Cataloging-in-Publication Data

Names: Machajewski, Sarah.
Title: Elon Musk / Sarah Machajewski.
Description: New York : PowerKids Press, 2018. | Series: Breakout biographies | Includes index.
Identifiers: ISBN 9781508160540 (pbk.) | ISBN 9781508160564 (library bound) | ISBN 9781508160557 (6 pack)
Subjects: LCSH: Musk, Elon–Juvenile literature. | Businesspeople–United States–Biography–Juvenile literature. | Businesspeople–South Africa–Biography–Juvenile literature.
Classification: HC102.5.M88 M33 2018 | DDC 332.1'78–dc23

Manufactured in China

CPSIA Compliance Information: Batch Batch #BS17PK: For Further Information contact Rosen Publishing, New York, New York at 1-800-237-9932

CONTENTS

STANDING OUT

Success means something different to everyone. It could mean getting a good grade, discovering something new, or becoming famous. A lot of people think money is a sign of success. There are countless ways to measure success, and people achieve it every day. But every once in a while, someone special comes along and breaks the mold. Elon Musk is one of these people.

An **engineer**, inventor, investor, and **entrepreneur**, Elon Musk began his spectacularly successful business career in the 1990s and became a multimillionaire by the age of 27. Musk's talents have influenced many industries and have transformed many **technologies** such as online payments and space travel. What they all have in common is Musk's **unique** vision—and his ability to turn innovation into amazing success.

Elon Musk, pictured here, has impacted how we interact with technology today.

WHAT IS INNOVATION?

Elon Musk is a breakout success because of his ability to innovate. Innovation means doing something in a new way or introducing a new idea. Innovation happens when someone thinks of how they can make something better or solve a problem. Imagine if you invented a robot to walk your dog. That's innovation at work!

Elon Musk is a great innovator because he takes creative ideas and turns them into actual products and solutions that change the way we do things. But what really makes him successful is that he's also an entrepreneur. An entrepreneur is a person who starts and leads a business. Entrepreneurs take big risks and work hard. Combined with his ability to innovate, Elon Musk's entrepreneurial spirit has paid off in a big way.

Elon Musk speaks at a conference about innovation. His experience and successes make many people eager to listen to what he has to say.

INNOVATIONS AROUND US

When you think about innovation, you may picture robots and computers. But some of the greatest innovations are simple, everyday items. Shoes, types of medicine, cars, toothbrushes, and toilets are innovations that have changed how we live. What's amazing about innovation is that there are no limits. If you want to innovate, think about a product you can improve. It all starts with a creative idea!

EARLY LIFE

Elon Musk was born on June 28, 1971, in Pretoria, South Africa. His mother, Maye, is Canadian. She has two master's degrees and is a dietician and a former model. Musk's father, Errol, is a South African pilot, sailor, and engineer.

Musk showed an interest in—and a talent for—computers early in his life. Musk's peers often bullied him because of his interests. He taught himself how to program. Programming is writing instructions, called code or software, that tell a computer how to function. Musk used his skills to create a video game called *Blastar*, which he sold to a computer magazine when he was just 12 years old! From an early age, it was clear that Musk had a knack for invention and entrepreneurship.

Elon Musk displayed his unique talents at a young age. His talent has taken him all the way to the international stage.

MAYE MUSK

9

ON TO COLLEGE

In 1989, when he was just 17 years old, Musk moved to Canada to attend college. He began classes at Queen's University in Kingston, Ontario. However, in 1992, he moved to Philadelphia, Pennsylvania, and began attending the University of Pennsylvania. He graduated in 1995 with bachelor's degrees in physics and economics.

Musk then moved to California to start graduate school at Stanford University. This move would change Musk's life. The Internet was growing, and it was creating jobs and plenty of opportunities for people interested in computers. The Internet boom was especially strong in California. Musk was in the right place at the right time. He dropped out of Stanford after two days and set his sights on a career that provides people with new technologies

Musk moved to California at the perfect time. The Internet was growing quickly, and there were plenty of opportunities to be a part of the boom.

THE INTERNET

The earliest **version** of the Internet started in the 1960s. However, most people became familiar with the Internet as we know it today in the 1980s. In the mid-1990s to late 1990s, many people invested heavily in Internet companies. Many well-known tech companies, including Google, were founded during this time. Elon Musk started his first companies during the Internet boom, and his great success soon followed.

THE FIRST BIG RISK

The same year Musk dropped out of Stanford, he founded his first company in Palo Alto, California. Zip2 produced software that provided maps and business directories (listings of names, addresses, and phone numbers) to newspapers for use on their websites. At the time, newspapers wanted to offer more online content, but they needed a way to help their readers find what they were looking for. Musk and his brother Kimbal, who cofounded Zip2, recognized a need for information—and met it.

Big newspapers like the *New York Times* and the *Chicago Tribune* used Zip2 to succeed in their new online environment. Musk's company became successful very quickly. In February 1999, a computer company called Compaq bought Zip2 for $307 million. Musk was a millionaire, and he

In 1998, Zip2 was set to join forces with CitySearch, another city guide company. This deal was valued at $300 million, but at the last second Musk and his brother backed out of the agreement.

KIMBAL MUSK

A SECOND STAB AT SUCCESS

With millions of dollars of **momentum** behind him, Musk set out to start his next company. He stayed in the tech industry. With the Internet becoming a stronger and more popular tool every day, there were many opportunities for entrepreneurs and innovators like Musk.

Musk used $10 million of the money he made from selling Zip2 to finance his next company. In 1999, he founded X.com, a financial services and payments company. X.com acted like an online bank through which people could send and receive money using e-mail addresses.

X.com gained the attention of investors because of Musk's record of success with Zip2. More importantly, it gained the attention of consumers. Within two months of its launch, X.com had 100,000 customers.

GETTING FUNDING

Investment capital is money from investors that's used to start or improve a business. Investors give entrepreneurs capital, or money, when they believe in an idea and think it will be successful. Entrepreneurs have to work hard to get funding. Having a good idea is one thing, but they have to prove it will be successful. Musk clearly had both things covered. X.com received millions of dollars in start-up capital from a leading investment firm in California.

Elon Musk holds an X.com credit card, which some customers used for the online payment service.

A BILLION-DOLLAR COMPANY

A company called Confinity quickly became X.com's competitor. Musk knew that in order to remain competitive, the two companies needed to join forces. X.com merged, or united, with Confinity in 2000. The new company was later renamed PayPal after one of Confinity's services.

PayPal is an online payment company that allows users to exchange money without using cash or checks. Users can send and receive money securely. After the merger, the company continued to increase in popularity. Musk served as PayPal's **chief executive officer (CEO)** for less than two years and eventually left that role to continue his entrepreneurial ventures.

In 2002, online auction company eBay purchased PayPal for $1.5 billion. At that time, Musk was the

PETER THIEL

PayPal

Elon Musk and Confinity cofounder Peter Thiel pose for a photo in 2000. This photograph was taken a few years before the company planned to **go public**.

Make your money go further with PayPal.

Accepted by millions of brands
Use PayPal at businesses, big and small, in 200+ countries around the world. Pay securely online, in apps, and in stores.

"MAKING LIFE MULTIPLANETARY"

Musk made millions off the sale of PayPal. His keen business sense and ability to innovate made him a pioneer in the Internet and tech worlds. But he soon switched his focus to another **frontier**—space.

This time, Musk's creativity went beyond the boundaries of Earth. He dreamed of a universe in which people could travel between planets and eventually live on them. But how would he achieve this dream? Musk set out to find a way to do this.

In 2002, Musk founded Space Exploration Technologies Corp. It's popularly known as SpaceX. Musk wants SpaceX to revolutionize space technology. Its first efforts were focused on making spacecraft for commercial, or for-profit, space travel. However, Musk's goal is to make it possible for people to live on other planets.

Musk speaks publicly about SpaceX's newest projects.

SPACEX
MAKES STRIDES

In an interview with *Investor's Business Daily*, Musk said, "I like to be involved in industries . . . that are changing the world. Space is one of those things." Musk said he tried to understand why space travel and exploration were so limited. He said, "As I dove into this, it seemed the [reason] was cost. The fundamental issue was reliable, low-cost access to space."

Musk directed his company to use the most **sophisticated** and lightweight materials available. SpaceX's first rocket to reach orbit, the *Falcon 1*, was launched in 2008. Since then, SpaceX has developed various spacecraft meant to shuttle supplies to the International Space Station (ISS). Musk's company has signed deals with NASA to fly supply missions—and eventually astronauts—to the ISS.

ROCKETING INTO THE FUTURE

In the summer of 2015, SpaceX made international news when a *Falcon 9* rocket exploded minutes after takeoff, destroying everything on board. SpaceX and Musk received a lot of bad press. Another *Falcon 9* spacecraft exploded on September 1, 2016. Musk's goal is to make sure all of SpaceX's spacecraft are safe enough for passenger travel.

Musk's quest to improve space travel is no small venture. But his creative vision, backed by his personal fortune, makes it possible for his dreams to become reality.

CHANGING CARS

Musk is also using his fortune to find creative solutions to the energy crisis. Alternative energy is energy created from resources that don't harm the environment. Solar and water power could one day replace harmful energy sources such as coal and natural gas, which are called fossil fuels. This is exactly what Musk set out to do when he got involved with Tesla Motors in 2004.

Founded in 2003 by a group of engineers in Silicon Valley, California, Tesla Motors designs and manufactures electric cars. In 2008, five years after the company's founding, Tesla released its first model: the Tesla Roadster. The Roadster has an electric motor with a rechargeable battery. It can travel 245 miles (394.3 km) on just one charge. Tesla sold 2,400 Roadsters to customers around

TESLA

The Tesla Roadster is an exciting innovation in the automobile industry.

NIKOLA TESLA

The Roadster's design was built around something rather old—a motor invented in 1888. Inventor Nikola Tesla designed a new type of electric motor. His invention was innovative for a time when people didn't fully understand **alternating current (AC)** electricity. We now do, thanks in part to Tesla. Tesla himself was a visionary, which is why it's no surprise that his technology is being used at one of today's most groundbreaking companies. His inventiveness inspired Tesla Motors' founders to name the company in his honor.

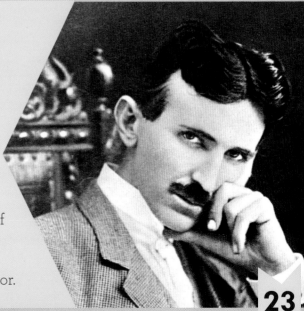

23

CONTINUING TO INNOVATE

Musk's talent for entrepreneurship and innovation brought him success once again. In June 2010, he led Tesla Motors to an **initial public offering** that raised $226 million for the company. In just over a decade, this was the fourth business he was involved in to earn millions of dollars.

The company's success was just beginning. In 2012, Tesla introduced its Model S, an electric car, which earned *Motor Trend's* 2013 Car of the Year award. While owners usually charge their cars at home, for long journeys they can use the Tesla Supercharger network. The company provides free high-speed charging stations along major routes in many countries. Tesla's goal is to make owning and operating its cars easy and convenient.

Tesla Motors continues to innovate and improve its products. Currently, it's working on a driverless car. Could that be the future of automobiles?

POWERING OUR HOMES

Musk supports alternative energy solutions by investing in companies that are searching for new ways to power our homes and businesses. In August 2016, Tesla Motors purchased a solar panel company called SolarCity for $2.6 billion. Solar panels absorb, or take in, sunlight and **convert** it into electricity.

Lyndon and Peter Rive, Musk's cousins, founded SolarCity in 2006. Musk serves as the chairman of the company and is also a major shareholder. Today, SolarCity is one of the biggest home solar panel companies in the United States. The company aims to be one of the biggest solar panel companies in the world, with a goal of making it easy for all people to use solar power.

LYNDON RIVE

PETER RIVE

One principle that unites all of Musk's current business ventures is his commitment to making innovative technologies less expensive.

LOOKING TOWARD THE FUTURE

Musk's career began in the late 1990s. In less than 20 years, he has been involved with several successful tech companies, some of which are worth billions of dollars. His companies have shaped young industries and forged paths into new ones. Musk has focused on developing products that help our world. He also works to spark our curiosity and desire to explore worlds beyond ours.

Musk is a driving force in the tech world. His talent for identifying opportunities and creating new ones is what has built his fortune. However, it's his innovation and visionary thinking that make him a breakout success story. What does the future hold for Elon Musk? If his track record of success is any indication, Elon Musk can accomplish anything he sets his mind to.

Elon Musk has become one of the world's great innovators.

TIMELINE

June 28, 1971	Elon Musk is born in South Africa.
1984	Musk creates a video game called *Blastar* and sells it to a computer magazine.
1989	Musk moves to Canada to attend college at Queen's University.
1992–1995	Musk attends the University of Pennsylvania.
1995	Musk founds Zip2 with his brother Kimbal.
1999	Compaq Computers buys Zip2 for $307 million. Musk becomes a millionaire. Musk founds X.com, his second company.
2000	X.com and Confinity merge to become PayPal.
2002	Online auction site eBay purchases PayPal for $1.5 billion. Musk founds SpaceX to revolutionize space travel and technology.
2004	Musk becomes involved with Tesla Motors, a company that produces electric cars.
2008	Tesla debuts the Tesla Roadster. It sells 2,400 of the cars. SpaceX launches the first privately owned, liquid-fueled rocket, the *Falcon 1*, into orbit.
2012	SpaceX's *Falcon 9* travels to the International Space Station.
2013	The Tesla Model S receives *Motor Trend's* Car of the Year award.
2015	One of SpaceX's *Falcon 9* spacecraft explodes seconds after takeoff.
2016	One of SpaceX's *Falcon 9* spacecraft explodes during a routine launchpad test. Tesla Motors acquires SolarCity, a solar panel company.

GLOSSARY

alternating current (AC): An electric current that reverses its direction at regular intervals.

chief executive officer (CEO): The person who has the most authority in an organization.

convert: To change from one thing into another.

engineer: To design and develop something using science or math or a person who is trained in or follows as a profession a branch of engineering.

entrepreneur: A person who organizes and operates a business.

frontier: A new field to be developed.

go public: To become a public company, such as when a company's stocks become available for purchase.

initial public offering: The first time stock of a private company is offered to the public.

momentum: The force that something has when it is moving.

shareholder: Someone who owns shares in a company or business.

sophisticated: Appealing to one's intelligence or very complicated.

technology: A method that uses science to solve problems and the tools used to solve those problems.

unique: Special or different.

version: One form of something.

INDEX

WEBSITES

Due to the changing nature of Internet links, PowerKids Press has developed an online list of websites related to the subject of this book. This site is updated regularly. Please use this link to access the list: www.powerkidslinks.com/bbios/musk